HIDDEN REALITIES

REAL TALK FOR WOMEN

D0921132

Letitia Austin

Printed in the United States of America

ISBN: 978-1-7333969-2-9

10 9 8 7 6 5 4 3 2 1

Empire Publishing and Literary Service Bureau

www.empirebookpublishing.com

Introduction
Letitia Austin

Let's be honest with ourselves. Life will take us to some places that will challenge us and literally move us out of our comfort zones. Whether it is our workplace, relationships, stagnate mindsets, or not being able to deal with grief.

Entering upon a new phase in my life was difficult as well as uncertain. As an educator who had been successful, and loved what I was doing, I truly believed that I was in a good place. Being recognized for the first time as "Teacher of the Year" and again within two years at the same school was phenomenal. At the time, I taught second grade at an elementary school in my hometown.

Like many teachers, I felt content just knowing that I was making a difference in so many young lives- the epitome of what the underprivileged students had dreamed their parents could be. Then, God orchestrated a plan for me to serve as a middle school teacher. I welcomed the challenge of moving from elementary to middle school. I taught for two years. Now, this "New phase" I am speaking of is a sudden offer to become the Lead Teacher then move up to Assistant Principal at a middle school. I was comfortable with the role of an assistant administrator until God demonstrated He had other plans for me..."Wow!" I thought, "Is this for me? "Is this something that I really want?" Before I could express my hesitation, my Pastor revealed in a sermon what God needed me to hear, "It's Your Turn."

Just when I thought I had adjusted, the principal at my school received a promotion. You're probably correct in your assumption to what occurred next. Suddenly, I had the astonishing task to make a decision of changing roles once again.

Now, I was to become the Principal of my place of employment, where I had finally adjusted to the best of my ability. So, yet again, I would need to welcome additional responsibility into my life. Although, not forced upon me, something within made me aware of an untiring capability and hidden desire to carryout God's plan for me.

Shockingly, I felt a sense of being in too deep. I knew that it would be frowned upon if I stepped away without a legitimate reason. I was actually doing quite well in my new role. Little did they know, I had to face a family at home that needed me more. Two children Taylor, a college student trying to find herself, her worth, and her purpose in life.

Then, Corbin, an upcoming high school freshman who needed me more than I could be available to him, due to the obligation and dedication to the 700 plus students and 89 staff members.

I often reflect on the familiar saying, "You see my Glory, but you don't know my Story." I know you're thinking, "Is there a male parent in the home?" Now, I will mention that my husband is present and also serves in an administrative role at a middle school in our hometown. Yes, there was double stress within the home. I was slowly led to a mild state of depression. My health was impacted greatly due to the demands of work. I needed to try to avoid a more severe state.

I don't know what came over me. Suddenly, I realized that I had accumulated tremendous responsibilities beyond my wildest imagination. What do you do when you are pushed into your purpose? What do you do when you are being stretched spiritually?

There are hidden realities that I discovered that must be unveiled in order for purpose to be realized.

Gratitude

Patricia:

You are a God send. I have no doubt that your connection to me is a Devine appointment. Your part in making my dream a reality is indeed purpose driven. I admire your gift and your humble spirit. You are a kind soul. I thank you from the depth of my mind, spirit and soul for your guidance and contribution.

Nicole:

Thank you dearly for being my friend. Your support when I needed it the most is much appreciated.
Our connection is divinely appointed.

Cassandra:

You have been my friend and supporter since elementary school. God has sustained our connection. I am forever thankful.

Pastor Wooden, Minister Brinson and my sisters in Christ:

Words cannot express my love and gratitude. Thank you for being part of my spiritual growth and journey.

To Michael, Taylor and Corbin

I love you...This is for you. Love covers all.

Mama, sisters and extended family:

I love you dearly. Thank you for your wisdom, advice, support and guidance on this journey.

Daddy:

I love and miss you. I wish you were here to be a part of this chapter in my life.

Contents

Chapter One

The Reality of Depression

Not me - the one with an exuberant personality, the one who loves to laugh, the one who brings joy to a room, the one who keeps the girls laughing. Not me - the one in the most professional arena, the one who looks almost flawless on the outside, the one who women approach for advice.

Not me - the one who executes faith, the one who keeps the family together, the one who helped raise Taylor and Corbin to have profound confidence, the one who keeps Michael happy, the one who has her mother's strength. Not me - the encourager and the motivator, the Teacher, the Assistant Principal and now the Principal, responsible for 700 plus students and 80 plus adults. Not me - the one who leads a ministry!

I can't seem to get the sleepless nights and the twists and turns out of my head! Have you ever dealt with your mind just running to no end? Do you feel like there is no way to collect your thoughts? Think about the rain as it pounds on a window. Can you hear that annoying sound of a clock, "tick tock, tick tock"? It never ends.

The worrying seems to overpower you, even when you know and understand the scriptures. In the book of Proverbs, chapter 3 verses 5-6 tells us to *"Trust in the Lord with all thine heart; and lean not unto thine own understanding."* Also, we are reminded that *"In all thy ways, we are to acknowledge Him, and He shall direct our paths.*" Just imagine trying to find answers to problems that only God can solve. What about giving it to God and declaring that you're going to let Him handle it? Then, you still don't see results. You naturally become anxious. You continue to cry out for help.

You constantly worry about everyday concerns. You begin to ask, "When can I clean?" "What about the bills?" "What about the never ending tasks at work?" Then, what do you do? You take a pill to try to get some sleep. Your mind is still running rapidly about normal everyday problems. This goes on for weeks, then months. All of the agony is commonly accompanied by physical symptoms such as chronic fatigue, headaches, muscle aches, sweating, and lightheadedness. Sometimes you're not sure if you are about to stroke out or have a heart attack!

So, then I began to ask myself, "Why not me?" God chose me to go through what most African American women repeatedly deny. Some form of a mental illness...Yes, Depression. So, now I realize...Yes, me.. Letitia Austin deals with Depression. Honestly, I really struggled with sharing this part of my life's story because it is both intimate and personal. However, I realize that we experience these struggles in order to help someone else. I pray that as I share my battle with Anxiety and Depression, that others are delivered and become more willing to share their stories as they become healed. I realize that this is not all about me, but being a blessing to others.

It all started when I was teaching at an elementary school. I considered it to be my most happy place. The joy of the little ones, I thought. I never really felt like I had a job. The reality is, I had an illness that I did not recognize. I was so happy that I did not allow myself to detect that anything was wrong. Then, suddenly, I started feeling anxious about the least little things. I started crying and having severe headaches. I remember having to leave work often - the place that I loved.

Yes, I remember the early signs. I also remember ignoring the signs, calling it fatigue or simply needing a change. I was too young to believe that I was actually dealing with Depression.

I literally went to see a doctor several years ago. He diagnosed me with "needing a new job." Believe it or not, within a year, I was in a new position. I loved it. I was happy for some time. The change was good. However, I still continued to experience anxiousness and symptoms that were unsettling.

Now, let's (you and me) examine several types of Depression:

By Nancy Schimelpfening | Medically reviewed by a board-certified physician

Updated January 16, 2019

"When people think about Depression, they often divide it into one of two things—either Clinical Depression which requires treatment, or "regular" Depression that pretty much anyone can experience. As a condition, Depression can be a difficult concept to grasp since we refer to it as both the symptom of a condition as well as the condition itself.

From a medical standpoint, Depression is defined as a mood disorder which causes a persistent feeling of sadness and often profound loss of interest in things that usually bring you pleasure. It affects how you feel, think, and behave and can interfere with your ability to function and carry on with your daily life.

There are many different causes of depression, some of which we don't fully understand. I will focus on the types. Some of the more common types include the following:

Major Depressive Disorder (MDD)

When people use the term Clinical Depression, they are generally referring to Major Depressive Disorder (MDD). It is a mood disorder characterized by a number of key features:

- Depressed mood

- Lack of Interest in activities normally enjoyed

- Changes in weight

- Changes in sleep

- Fatigue

- Feelings of worthlessness and guilt

- Difficulty concentrating

- Thoughts of Death and Suicide

If a person experiences the majority of these symptoms for longer than a two-week period, they will often be diagnosed with MDD.

Persistent Depressive Disorder

Dysthymia, now known as Persistent Depressive Disorder, refers to a type of chronic depression present for more days than not for at least two years. It can be mild, moderate, or severe.

Bipolar Disorder

Bipolar Disorder is a mood disorder characterized by periods of abnormally elevated moods known as mania. These periods can be major, can be mild (hypomania) or they can be extreme enough to cause marked impairment within a person's life, require hospitalization, or affect a person's sense of reality. The vast majority of those with bipolar illness also have episodes of major depression. Researchers believe that it is possible that a tendency towards

- Extreme fatigue

- Feeling sad, hopeless, or self-critical

- Severe feelings of stress or anxiety

- Mood swings, often with bouts of crying

- Irritability

- Inability to concentrate

- Food cravings or binging

Hormonal treatments may be necessary in addition to antidepressants and major lifestyle changes.

Seasonal Affective Disorder (SAD)

This is the type of Depression that I most closely identify. If you experience depression, sleepiness, and weight gain during the winter months but feel perfectly fine in spring, you may have a condition known as Seasonal Affective Disorder (SAD), currently called Major Depressive Disorder, with seasonal pattern.

SAD is believed to be triggered by a disturbance in the normal circadian rhythm of the body. Light entering through the eyes influences this rhythm, and any seasonal variation in night/day pattern can cause a disruption leading to Depression.

SAD is more common in far northern or far southern regions of the planet and can often be treated with light therapy to offset the seasonal loss of the daylight."

Often times I think God allowed me to go through Depression to better understand what my mother-in-law was experiencing. She suffered from Depression for years. I can remember when she was dealing with a severe case for eight years with no sign of healing until one day God intervened and she was delivered. She shares her testimony freely.

Let me be clear, I tried to remain strong. Black women in-particular are supposed to be strong. As years past, I began to work in leadership. I put on a glorified persona. I had to be the strong black woman. You know, we have to work harder and stronger.

As black women, we must understand how Black women are viewed in this country. These images affect how other people see Black women and how we see ourselves. They also play a role in the development and maintenance of anxiety. According to author, Dr. Angela Neal-Barnett, a professor of Psychological Sciences and director of the Program for Research on Anxiety, Strong Black Women are legendary. Harriet Tubman, Sojourner Truth, and all Black grandmothers are renowned for their persistence and perseverance.

There are many positive aspects about being a Strong Black Woman, but there are negatives as well. We are the ones who are expected to fail at any admirable endeavor. A Strong Black Woman "keeps on keeping on" even when she knows she should stop, placing her mental and physical health at risk.

Executive wellness coach and physician, Carol J. Scott M.D., chimes in on the reality of negative health impacts brought on by race-related discrimination among black women in her Huffington Post article: "Stress, Health and African American Women: A Black History Month Notation".

She cites research that provides evidence of how subtle mistreatment over time leads to increased surges in Diastolic Blood Pressure (DBP) for African American women. She also addresses the alarming rates of ambulatory medical visits and incidences of strokes and deaths in hypertensive black women compared to other ethnicities.

I was a first year principal. I could no longer ignore the signs. My job was demanding. God had placed me in a position that stretched me to no end. My inner strength was being stretched. My spiritual being was being stretched. My health was at risk. When I drove up to the school, I felt an overwhelming amount of stress and anxiety. The emotional toll it had on me was indescribable. I was responsible for so many lives. At the same time I had to be both effective and impactful.

The reality is that principals experience anxiety when they anticipate situations which are likely to worsen. As the principal of the school, I had to exercise coping strategies and focus on my divine assignment in order to maintain my sanity. Not only was my health at risk, but my students and staff were also at risk. I could not give in nor give up. I had to rely on my support system.

According to ESG, Employee Staffing Group (2019) so many of us are torn between juggling heavy workloads, managing relationships and family responsibilities, and squeezing in outside interests, it's no surprise that more than one in four Americans describe themselves as "Super Stressed." And that's not balanced—or healthy.

In our rush to "get it all done" at the office and at home, it's easy to forget that as our stress levels spike our productivity plummets. Stress can zap our concentration, make us become irritable or depressed, and harm our personal and professional relationships.

It happened to me my first year as principal. I remember it so well. I was trying to fight depression and anxiety with prayer and faith, but I needed help. It was then when the doctor prescribed my first dose of medicine for anxiety. I started feeling better within two weeks. I could function normally. I had my smile again. I could laugh.

Even if I wanted to worry, I did not worry. I was able to walk in my faith. My head was up. I welcomed challenges. I was what I am sometimes called by some of my friends... "Diva." Again... I will always remember the words of a former Dean at my Alma Mater, Albany State University. He would always emphasize the quote by William H. Johnson, *"If it is to Be, It is up to Me."*

Note of Reflection:

*Author Michelle McKinney Hammond in her book, Release the Pain, Embrace the Joy emphasizes that there is only one way to find the right answer to all your questions, and that is to talk to the One who knows. God is a perfect gentleman; He will not answer until we ask. He will not give His opinion without invitation. He will not touch us until we draw near. Prayer is the most necessary ingredient in the salve of healing. All attempts are impotent without it. She reminds us; in spite of your weariness, in spite of your depression, in spite of your feelings of hopelessness - in spite of it all, **Pray.***

Chapter Two

The Reality "Behind the Makeup"

Every morning, I put on my makeup. It's perfect double wear by Clinique. It covers well, all day in fact. I then add my concealer; It hides the blemishes well. Now the eyeliner, blush and mascara; you know it makes my eyes appear to be wide open. Now, it's all perfect. No one will be able to distinguish the days when I am really tired. I put on my usual cute sassy dresses. I like them a bit above the knee. I top it all off with some kind of perfume, one that my sister provides me with. It's the perfect birthday gift every year.

I set out to face the world, and all of the looks, the faces, the perceptions - the world and its standards. I have this permanent smile, one that shows up in all my pictures. There she is, Letitia Austin. *"The Woman to Watch,"* according to "Bainbridge Living Magazine" (2013). I even made the front cover. I often remind myself that no one knows your story but they see your glory. This was one of my most accomplishments of which I am most proud. I did not see it coming. However, I realized others saw something in me.

My story was about my journey as an educator, my journey as a woman, my values, my beliefs, and my leadership. There it was, all in print, professional photography and all. It was written in a way that most of Bainbridge could read all about Letitia Austin. "What an accomplishment!" I thought. I remember the interview with the professional photographer for the magazine. She asked questions like, "Where did you grow up? Where did you get your foundation? We decided to photograph me in front of the church where I started my spiritual foundation.

Why do women wear makeup?

According to Vanessa Van Edwards, an estimated 44 percent of American women do not like to leave their homes without makeup. Research shows there are two primary reasons why women wear makeup:

1) Camouflage– Women who are anxious and insecure tend to use makeup to appear less noticeable.

2) Seduction– Women who want to be noticeably more attractive tend to use makeup to be more confident, sociable and assertive.

Women have it drilled into them from a young age that to be successful in everything from dating to job interviews, to forming friendships with other popular girls, they need to be pretty, and the basis for that isn't entirely cultural. It may not be fair, but according to the Association for Psychological Science, attractive people are treated more favorably in every area of life, from dating, to jobs, and even to criminal trials. Take a minute to think about someone that you find physically beautiful. It can be a friend of yours or a celebrity. What makes them beautiful in your eye? Is it flawless skin, or is it a twinkle in their eyes? Is it due to a kindness they possess that oozes from their essence? What qualities do you find attractive that arise from inside beauty?

Some time ago, I spoke at a local church for a Women's Day program. God gave me the words to share from the topic, "Beauty in the Eyes of God." I spoke specifically about what the Word says in Psalm 139:14

"I praise you because I am fearfully and wonderfully made; your works are wonderful; I know that full well."

This means;

You are created in the image of God. He sees you as a masterpiece; and when you look in the mirror, He wants you to "know that full well." Try this beauty tip: Every morning when you look in the mirror, say Psalm 139:14 and smile. You might even tape the verse on your mirror as a reminder!

I have done just that before. Allow me to remind you of the Reality - You don't know what I am thinking behind the smile, behind my demeanor. I am sure I am thinking what most women think. Who am I? What am I doing? Who am I hiding from behind the makeup? Let me be real. I cannot hide from who I am, what I think, what I believe and what I deal with on my spiritual journey. I can only tell you that I trust God with my life. I believe He will continue to guide me as I deal with me.

I didn't mention it before, but I'm rather small in stature. I stand only 5' 1". There is probably only one student in the entire school who is actually shorter than I am. Even among my coworkers and colleagues, I sometimes feel inferior. Often, I wish I was taller. Therefore, it is helpful for me to put forth a special effort to make my presence known. I tend to wear heels to get that extra boost. However, I can still be powerful, regardless of my size. You see, God knows us well. He knows our inner thoughts and most importantly, our heart. He sees what is on the inside no matter how much it is camouflaged. He knows the heart.

Elizabeth George points out in her book, Beautiful in God's Eyes, many women do the chores at home because they have to, they are expected to, or told to do them. But the woman, who is beautiful in God's eyes, throws herself wholeheartedly into her work. She rises above the world's demands. She sets a worthy example and finds pleasure in the work of her hands. She is beautiful from the inside.

A woman who is beautiful from the inside;

Prays daily - She prays for her attitude, her heart and the way she responds to others.

Values each day - She strives to achieve excellence in God's eyes.

Protects her identity - She is cautious. She watches her steps and tastes her words.

Has a vision for loveliness - God's beautiful woman appreciates beauty and its ministry to those it touches.

Finally, she surrounds herself with beauty. She spends time with people who create beauty and those who exude beauty. She enjoys being among people who are positive. Also, she appreciates those who pour into her as well as those who want to see her become great.

Chapter Three

The Reality of When Your Circle Gets Smaller

It is real. Think about it. As you get older, life brings about many changes. For years, I was careful about who I allowed in my circle. People are seasonal and God wastes no experiences. I count it a blessing to still have childhood and college friends. The reality is God will show you who He wants to be in your life through experiences.

I heard one preacher's sermon, "Just keep Living." People will show you who they are. The reality is stop trying to figure people out, they will reveal themselves in time.

I can remember when God challenged and transitioned me into roles and circumstances where I learned quickly who was for me and who was against me. More importantly, I learned that it was not people, but the spirit working behind the people to disrupt my focus and purpose. People will reveal themselves in so many ways. They are fashioned in different shapes, sizes and races. They come from all walks of life. They can be friends, family, co-workers, or even people you confide in. Believe me, they will be revealed. They are many times hidden, but life experiences expose their identity and true intentions.

Let me be real, as we are elevated in life, some people cannot handle your ascension. God has brought you to this point in your life and He alone will allow you to continue your journey. One of my favorite quotes is;

"Never apologize for having high standards. People who really want to be in your life will rise up to meet them." ~**Anonymous**

14

Allow me to get personal, as God transitioned me or elevated me at various stages of life, I suddenly began to notice that others were intimidated and detached even though I remained the same. You see, I am not moved by titles nor elevations. It is forever my goal to remain humble and grateful. I must mention the fact that I also accumulated several of those who are often referred to as "Haters." These are the ones who for some reason or another cannot be genuinely happy for others and their accomplishments or achievements. This also defines their spirits.

Sometimes, I felt myself feeling sad and lonely when my circle of friends became smaller and smaller as I grew older. But, I am one to exercise my wisdom and totally understand that God wants to bless me and will send the right people in my life.

However, I am aware that there are those who are negatively fixated on my success and their lack of progress. I cannot allow my spirits to be dampened due to focusing on things that do not positively enhance my life. I have to continue to be spiritual and I will always be content as I am being lifted or elevated in life.

I also understand that it is completely normal to lose friends as you grow in wisdom. I am making a very clear distinction between friendships, co-workers, colleagues, and my social circle. I am constantly assessing, "What do they want from me?" "What can they bring to my life?"

I remember teaching a class at church in the Empowerment class from the book, "Right People Right Place Right Plan" by Jentzen Franklin. In one chapter, he discusses quite thoroughly, "Character Discernment." This speaks volumes to my life. Romans 8:5 says *Those who* live according to the flesh set their minds on the things of the flesh, but those who live according to the Spirit, the things of the Spirit."

When some people come into your life, they do not just bring their bodies, they bring their spirits. He pointed out there are two types of people, flesh people and faith people. How can we identify flesh people? They tear you down and feed your fears. They get joy out of seeing you down. They only deposit negativity while faith people build you up and feed your faith.

I am especially thankful for a few genuine friends in my life. They are prayer partners, family, church members, Pastors and even a co-worker who I found to be a sincere friend. I hold them dear to my heart. They know me. I know them. My spirit of discernment confirms the true spirit in them. I am forever indebted. As a Christian, I can sometimes feel drained of emotional energy from being around people who I know I cannot trust, those who set out to harm and tear me down.

I am most thankful for my personal relationship with God as He keeps me grounded and rooted so that I can surpass the ignorance and the pettiness of fleshly spirits. Let me be clear, God wants us to love all those we come into contact with, but we have to make sure we surround ourselves with more people who fill our lives than drain our lives.

Allow me to share a reality. I was elevated professionally in a leadership capacity. Immediately, I felt lonely. I was always told that it is lonely at the top. It did not take me long to realize it.

I quickly realized that I could no longer hide in my comfort zone.

I had to depend on God and only God to help me through this place of uncertainty. I was almost sure I could count on the people around me. This was not so. I quickly realized that God was preparing me for MY DESTINY and that those around me were only seasonal.

I would hope for encouragement and even a pat on the back. Instead I was expected to deliver 100 percent, give all I had to give, encourage others, smile when I felt like crying, and treat others with love and respect, even though I knew I was not getting it in return.

It was draining, but at the same time rewarding, because I knew God had me on assignment. I knew I had to press my way and most importantly, stand for Christ and BE more like him. I had to hang on to the ones who I trust with my emotions and value their truth.

The reality concerning women and friendships is profound. A study by Laura Klein and Shelley Taylor on relationships between friendships and stress discovered that women react to stress differently than men. This is due to the amount of hormones that are released into the bloodstream. When men and women are stressed, the hormones cortisol and epinephrine are released together, which raise a person's blood pressure and circulating sugar level. Then oxygen comes into play, which counters the production of cortisol and epinephrine which produces a feeling of calm, reduces fear, and counters some of the negative effects of stress.

Taylor contends that women, on the other hand, are genetically hardwired for friendships in large part due to oxytocin released into their bloodstream, combined with female reproductive hormones. So, women seek out friendships with other women as a means of regulating stress levels.

The reality is sometimes a friendship does not support us in the way we need. When a friendship consistently leaves you feeling worse after spending time together, it might be time to reconsider the value of that friendship. Les Brown expressed it another way. He stated, "People inspire you, or they drain you. Pick them wisely." He also stated, "Accept responsibility for your life. Know that it is you who will get you where you want to go, no one else." I leave you with a few tips about the reality of friendship circles:

*Pray for God to send you faith people.

*Exercise your gift of discernment.

*Assess the people in your circle.

*Understand people are seasonal.

*Know that you are responsible for your personal growth.

Scriptures:

Proverbs 18:24 - "A man that hath friends must shew himself friendly: and there is a friend that sticketh closer than a brother.

Proverbs 13:20 – "He that walketh with wise men shall be wise: but a companion of fools shall be destroyed.

Proverbs 12:26 - "The righteous is more excellent than his neighbour: but the way of the wicked seduceth them.

1 Samuel 16:7 - "But the Lord said unto Samuel, Look not on his countenance, or on the height of his stature; because
I have refused him: for the Lord seeth not as man seeth; for man looketh on the outward appearance, but the Lord looketh on the heart.

1 Thessolonians 5:21 – "Prove all things; hold fast that which is good.

Chapter Four

The Reality of Grief

According to The American Psychological Association's article entitled "Grief: Coping with the Loss of Your Loved One," (March '2011), some point in our lives, we have either experienced or will experience some form of loss. Whether it's a friend or family member, this may be one of the hardest challenges that many of us will ever face. When we lose a spouse, sibling, or parent, our grief can be significantly intense. We know that loss is a natural part of life, but we can still be overcome by shock and confusion, leading to prolonged periods of sadness or even depression.

The sadness typically diminishes in intensity as time passes, but such feelings are overcome by the actual grieving process. At the same time, we must continue to embrace the time that we had with our loved ones.

Everyone reacts differently to death and employs personal coping mechanisms for grief. Research shows that most people can recover from loss on their own through the passage of time if they have social support and practice healthy habits. It may take months or even years to come to terms with a loss. Most importantly, there is no "normal" time period for someone to grieve.

According to The American Psychological Association's article entitled "Grief: Coping with the Loss of Your Loved One," (March '2011), grieving individuals may find it useful to use some of the following strategies to help come to terms with loss:

- Talking about the death of your loved one with friends and colleagues in order to understand what happened might relieve some of the grief. Some might have actually known your friend or family member. Denying the death is an easy way to isolate yourself, and will frustrate your support system in the process.

- It is okay to accept your feelings. People experience all kinds of emotions after the death of someone close. Sadness, anger, frustration, and even exhaustion are all normal.

You should focus on taking care of yourself and your family. Eating well, exercising, and getting plenty of rest will certainly help us get through each day. Then, we will be able to move forward.

- It is helpful for us to reach out and help others who are dealing with a loss. Helping others will have the added benefit of making you feel better as well.

- Sharing stories of the deceased can help you cope as you reminisce the life of your loved one.

- Possibilities include donating to a favorite charity of the deceased, framing photos of fun times, passing on a family name to a baby or planting a garden in loving memory.

- What you choose is up to you, as long as it allows you honor that unique relationship in a way that feels right for you.

- If you feel stuck or overwhelmed by your emotions, it may be helpful to talk with a licensed psychologist or other mental health professional who can help you cope with your feelings and find ways to get back on track.

I can remember it like it was yesterday. That phone call...the one no one wants to get. It was June 9, 2014. My mom called for me to pick her up to take her to the hospital. My dad had been at the nursing home just for a few weeks for therapy. He hated it. However, he needed to be there. My mom needed rest. She had recently undergone surgery as well. That morning was so quiet and unpredictable. I went to pick up my mom immediately.

We made it to the hospital. We were greeted by my uncle. I knew then... It was not good. I started screaming. My mom started crying. We both knew... We walked in the room. There he laid. Looking just like himself... that smile. I will never forget it. He left us with a beautiful smile.

He was such a gentle man. He was at peace. My mom made calls to get my sisters to return back home for this difficult season we were experiencing. It was the most difficult situation to digest. My uncle was so comforting. He never left us through the entire process.

We stayed at the hospital, for hours. My Pastor came to visit. He was right by my side. I finally got enough nerve and strength to call Michael. He came immediately. The most difficult part was when my Pastor and my best friend came with us to tell Taylor and Corbin. The grief was so intense for my mom, my children, and my sisters.

We were finally all gathered at the Hospital. Once they rolled him out, it all became so real. Then, we all met at my mom's house. My sister's friend showed up. My best friend and my pastor never left my side. We had so many people that reached out and showed support. My entire church family, my sisters' church family, and two very supportive friends stayed right by my side. I will always cherish the list of relatives and friends and all the condolences. The support was unbelievable.

For my mom, the sadness and loneliness was just as painful as losing my dad. She was so torn. They were married for 51 years. We had just celebrated one year before he passed. The reality of grief is indescribable. It changes you for life. It is a continuous process. Time heals, but grief lingers forever.

For some time, I knew that the day would come when I would most likely lose a parent rather than me leaving this world first. However, when the reality sets in, it still seems unreal. If you have lost someone you love, you should be prepared for the reality that grief will drag you through lots of emotions, including the loneliness, isolation and longing for your loved one that never quite go away. Sometimes you will feel comforted one day, then lost the next.

Grieving can be complex. Understanding the process of grieving is essential to understanding your emotions. We must understand that grieving can lead to a path of destruction if we are not careful when dealing with our emotions.

Personally, I did not understand the process of grief at that time. I was going through a whirlwind of emotions. I was so thankful that I visited my dad everyday at the nursing home, except that Sunday before he passed. My mom spent time with him. That time was meant for her. I cried almost every day. No one understood my pain. I found myself getting angry because no one seemed to hurt as bad as I did. Little did I know and understand, my mom had it worst than all of us.

I had to watch her go through depression. Then I watched her exude profound strength. I find myself reflecting back to the funeral service. It was so beautiful. The yellow ties, white dresses, and beautiful flowers I can still visualize them. My husband, Michael, sang so beautifully. My brother-in-law spoke so profoundly. Daddy would have been so proud of his profound words. I could see him smiling. The whole family was there reminiscing on how he made our lives so complete.

There was added sadness in our spirits, just knowing that my dad wouldn't be able to see my sister's unborn child. However, my sister had her baby girl just a few days after my dad's birthday. She is a beautiful child. We like sharing stories with her about my dad. Many times I think about how Daddy would have loved to see all of his grandchildren and great-grands grow up. They are all very special and I am sure he would be proud of them.

The day after the funeral seemed like the hardest day ever. The support was still there, but so far away. I would sometimes just sit and listen to music. l can remember playing "Millions," by the Winans. This was like a sense of peace for me. My dad was in Heaven. He made it! I knew it. I could feel it in my spirit. Then, suddenly I began to experience the grief process. I had already gone through denial, bargaining, anger and now finally, acceptance. (The 5 stages of death and dying).

This is the phase where you learn to accept the loss and allow it to become a part of your life. It is not so much that you are fine with the loss. Instead, your mind, body and emotions are finally able to accept what has occurred, and you see it as something you can absorb into your everyday life, thoughts and feelings.

My mom naturally has a very quiet demeanor. Sometimes, my sisters and I would be concerned as to whether she was okay. Often she didn't seem as emotional as we were or thought she should be about her loss. Being spiritual, she felt comfort in just knowing that my dad is "in a better place."

As time passed, she would not mention my dad as much. We were somewhat hesitant about questioning her, but it would be revealed in conversations with others. She would express, "I have my moments." We were content in realizing that she was coping in her own way.

Julie Chen discussed, "Accepting and Embracing Grief." In her article, she stated that Acceptance is evident when one is able to be at peace with what has happened and to be able to look forward to the future without pain or sadness.

I have done just that. As I write this, I am by no means healed by my grief from losing my dad. The ultimate question is always, "Why?" Constantly, I recognize the reality of having to let go. However, I have come to a place of genuine acceptance and peace.

Prayer for grief: Dear heavenly Father, my comforter, I ask that you continue to hold me close. As my tears fall, that you replace them with understanding that this too shall pass. I pray that you release joy in place of sorrow. I pray that you provide a sense of peace and fulfillment to replace the loss of my loved one. Like David, "my tears have been my food day and night" (Psalm 42:3). For however long this season of sorrow lasts, I pray that you would show me more of your love and grace. Amen

Chapter Five

Suppression is NOT in the Healing Process

In an article by Gay and Kathlyn Hendricks, it is emphasized that the world of feeling is unpredictable, confusing, and hard to control. That is, the nature of feeling. . . . Some people are fortunate enough to grow up in families that teach that it is acceptable to experience feelings and tell the truth about them. Many families -- perhaps most -- teach their children strategies that become problems for us later.

Often times I find myself suppressing feelings and emotions. I often ask myself, "Who can I talk to?" Of course my spouse, Michael, is always available. He is my best friend, my confidant, my soul mate, and my life partner. I constantly wonder if I could possibly worry him or add to his stress by constantly unloading on him. I love his strength and his level of faith. This is what I admire the most.

Michael is always there to offer encouragement and doesn't hesitate to boost my level of confidence as well. The reality is... I often wonder if he is actually listening attentively. I know he is actively listening and desires to hear me out. Because of this, I sometimes suppress my real feelings. I do have a few close friends that I can confide in for support.

However, I know this to be true; People will allow you to be stuck on silence. They tend to care more about you as the professional than an actual person. I also know and understand that silence and suppression cannot help you to heal.

We need to invest in our healing and not our feelings. Many times, I find myself just merely functioning. I now understand that in order to heal I need to eliminate everything that makes me ill. Most of us only bandage our problems rather than actually heal our wounds.

Often times, we deal with issues that we don't talk about and it negatively impacts our inner beings. Allow me to focus on three silent things that people deal with:

I. Finances

We have all been there: We can't sleep. We are worried about our finances. We worry about how to pay the bills. We are constantly adding it up in our heads, so much that we can't sleep. In fact, we lose sleep which can then lead to Insomnia. I have been there many nights. I wake up in a panic, trying to figure it all out. Then I find myself in a cold sweat. This is due to me suppressing the issue of finances. I soon realize that I had to deal with my fears and not allow my finances to negatively impact my health. In fact, I had to take control.

I can remember years ago, I would pack my bills along with my vacation clothes. I can hear Michael now, saying, "Where are you going with those bills?" I can write about it now, but years ago, it was a reality.

II. Spiritual Relationship with Christ.

We have to ensure that we do not allow ourselves to become disconnected from the Father. We have to remember, our connection to people is secondary. Christ must be first. Jennifer Sum addresses the suppression of emotions in her Dec. 5, 2017 article in Teaching "Humble Hearts;" on "Emotional Suppression is Ungodly and Harmful." She reminds us that the Bible teaches that God has given us appropriate times to express all our emotions. We simply need the emotional maturity to realize the right time to express the negative ones. She refers to Ecclesiastes 3:1, 3-4 ESV: *"For everything there is a season, and a time for every matter under heaven: ...a time to weep, and a time to laugh; a time to mourn and a time to dance."*

Sum also points out the fact that Self-Control is a good thing because it allows us to choose when and how we release our emotions. She further states that Emotional Suppression, on the other hand, will not release our emotions at all but allow them to remain hidden instead. Therefore, no matter how hard we try to suppress the negative emotions they can linger forever and ultimately destroy us.

Sum also included a few signs of suppressed emotions. If we recognize ourselves in at least two of them, then we must be willing to confront the issues so that we can finally move on with our lives. Among them are:

- Do we live with simmering anger, annoyance or contempt, and don't know why?

- Do we find it difficult to smile or laugh genuinely?
- Do we tear up or cry easily?
- Do we struggle with depression, despair, or sadness?

We also must consider questions in regard to our bodies:

- Do we constantly feel weary or fatigued?
- Do we find it hard or impossible to enjoy deep, restful sleep?

Finally, in regard to our relationship with God, we should ask ourselves the following:

- Do we pray intellectually and not from our hearts?
- Do we believe that God is good, but don't "feel" it?

Let you and I focus on the following scriptures.

Anger – Proverbs 29:11; Romans 1:18; Ephesians 4:26-31; Colossians 3:8; Proverbs 15:18

Laughter – Psalm 37:13; Job 7:21; Psalm 126:2; Ecclesiastes 2:2

Compassion – Exodus 33:19; Isaiah 30:18; Lamentations; Deuteronomy 32:36

Grief – Genesis 6:6; Romans 7:28; John 14:1; Philippians 4:6-8

Love – John 3:16; 1 Corinthians 16:14; 1 Peter 4:8; 1 John 4:18-19

III. Health

Do you realize you can suffocate in silence? It is not healthy to suppress your emotions or to keep what troubles you bottled up inside. You can become imprisoned in your own body.

You may start to have serious health issues. It is true and it actually happened to me. I can remember becoming overwhelmingly stressed and thought that no one would understand what I was going through. I was dealing with anxiety, and began to have other health issues that were surprising to me at such a young age. I now realize that if you are not healthy, you will not be any good to anyone. I have learned to take care of myself. I had to make a life-changing decision that impacted my family and my profession. It was a difficult decision but one that I had to make for the betterment of my well-being. It was a decision that others did not understand. You see, I am not concerned by the world's standards. I am only concerned about how I can make myself available to God so that I can be used by Him. Before I made the decision to move from one place to another in my profession, I prayed about it. I trusted God and only God with this one. I knew that I could not continue to work at the pace I was working. It was

30

unhealthy for me physically and spiritually. I was feeling bound and I knew I had to let go of something in order to be free in my spirit and back to a healthy place.

Finally, Roger Ebert revealed in an article, "This is Exactly How Suppressed Emotions Rule Your Life and 5 Ways to Change It," that emotions are an inseparable companion on life's journey every moment. Of course, there is no way to escape from them. Yet, many of us are unwilling to deal with them.

Every day, I meet people who try to get over some unwelcomed emotions. Instead of allowing themselves to feel whatever it is that they are feeling, they try to get over it. They are eating over it, thinking over it, shopping over it, and even working over it.

Ebert tells us that we must be present to our pain and be willing to break those comfortable patterns. We should not silence the pain. He tells us to give it sound by letting it out. We are programmed and conditioned to keep it in. There is another way. He reminds us that we need to let it out if we want to remain healthy.

Chapter Six

The Reality of Depositing into Your Children

At some point, all of us have asked this very important question. "Can parents have important and long-term effects on the development of their children?" My answer is "Absolutely, Yes!"

More specifically, as GloZell Green reminds us what parenting should represent, she explains that it is not about giving your children everything they want. Also, parenting is not being their friend. She emphasizes that parenting is about preparing your children to become useful and respectful in society.

As parents, we have to be careful about the messages we deposit into our children. Every facial expression, gesture, act and every single word from our mouth speak volumes to our children. Parenting requires a great deal of patience, wisdom, and love. They see us and learn from us. We are their first teachers. We condition them. Whether we realize it or not, often times they mimic us. And most importantly, our children look up to us.

However, we can help them make decisions about life by the way we live. My husband and I made many sacrifices in our lives so that our children could have the best education and the best opportunities possible. We, along with their grandparents and Aunts, decided that we would all make sacrifices for them. Our parents have blessed our children in many ways. They have been more than grandparents to them. They have provided them with guidance they will help them through life experiences. My sisters have been more than aunts to our children. They have helped us to rear them. They sow into their lives spiritually and financially. They have enriched their lives immensely.

I can remember it like it was yesterday when we introduced our first born to God. We talked to her about having a personal relationship with the Lord. She understood and accepted Christ at an early age. She was around seven years old. As she refers to 2 Timothy 1:7 NIV, *"For the Spirit God gave us does not make us timid, but gives us power, love and self-discipline,"* Taylor now lives a God Fearing life and even shares the Gospel with others.

She knows the Lord for herself. She knows how to trust in Him. I remember telling her that mommy and daddy will not always be around and that she needed to live to satisfy the Lord, not us. Taylor also knows and understands the words from 1 Samuel 2:9 which remind her that *"He will protect his faithful ones, but the wicked will disappear in darkness..."*

Our second born, Corbin, also accepted Christ at an early age. He is inquisitive and therefore, he asks many questions. We had to be ready to answer all of his questions about spirituality. Thankfully, he has a personal relationship with Christ. He studies often and also lives a God Fearing life.

God has blessed him with many gifts and talents. We always encourage him to use his gifts to the glory of God and his abilities or talents to help others in various capacities. We as parents are to "Rejoice in God's creation and the uniqueness found in each of our children." (cbn.com)

Corbin's humility will be rewarded in each endeavor. The Word states in 1 Samuel 2:1-2, 8-10, *"He gives power to his king; he increases the strength of his anointed one."* Whether it is through his paintings, his speaking, or his designs, we continuously encourage Corbin to let his light shine through. I knew he was a Believer when he suffered an illness for some time. He trusted God for his healing. We prayed with him daily. Our Pastor prayed with him and sent him encouraging words often while he was going through the process. Our son never gave in. I remember him saying out loud, "I believe."

You see, it is essential that parents teach their children about having a personal relationship with the Savior.

We must realize that our children are a gift from God. The Bible reveals to us a plan for parenting our children. Our children will experience challenges in life that their parents are unable to save them.

When I say "God Fearing" What I mean by that is; living in direct respect for God and His Word. This is a way that pleases God. We teach our children to be respectful and obedient to God's will and ways. Godly fear is not the same fear that one may experience when feeling afraid. To fear God is also to stand before Him in all we do in order to be pleasing to Him without allowing ourselves to be influenced by wanting the good opinion of people. The reality is, although we teach our children to be God-fearing, we understand that they may make decisions that are not pleasing to God. However, as parents, we must teach Godly ways of living.

God wastes no experiences. As much as parents would like to save their children from the tough times, this is impossible. Unfortunately, they will have to go through in order to grow and develop spiritually. "Each day of our lives we make deposits in the memory banks of our children." – (Charles R. Swindoll, Pastor and Author.)

I love watching my children grow. I love when they share the word with others. More importantly, I love when they pour back into us by sometimes sharing the Word and witnessing to us as parents. There have been many times when they became the encouragers. This is so rewarding.

I would say that the exposure to values and beliefs would be one of the strongest influences that parents have over the lives of their children. The manner in which parents expose their children to values or ideas becomes extremely important for children over time. At the same time, if parents teach values that oppose the negative influences of society, it increases the likelihood that their children might embrace these values and ultimately choose the right path.

There are many ways that parents can influence their children; one of two things has a tendency to occur: Some children choose to pattern themselves after what they witness their parents doing. Others choose to avoid being anything like their parents.

Parents are the child's first teacher. They impact the lives of their children greatly. Although children inherit traits from their parents, the environment that parents create is what their children are most likely to mimic.

By the same token, we as women have always been driven to provide a good home life and spiritual nurturance while rearing our children. Although most would prefer a supportive husband in the home, this is not always the case. The genuine love and guidance of the mother is what ultimately influences the degree of spirituality desired for her children. Therefore, it is very important for our relationship with the Lord to be at its best.

We will need the strength to be able to provide for them, both spiritually and emotionally. Although some children may deviate from their upbringing as they get older, the initial foundation of the mother will overpower some of the decisions and situations that they will encounter throughout life. However, we must be consistent with our guidance. It takes continuous prayer and supplication to make a lasting impression on our children.

So, yes we must have a genuine prayer life intact. However, we must be prepared for life's challenges. What do we do if our children go astray? What do we do when it seems like our rearing was in vain. We remember the sleepless nights when they were either out late or with friends that didn't quite meet our approval. Yes, we continue to pray.

The reality is that we never feel that our rearing is done. We continue to make sacrifices to provide whatever our children may need in regards to not only tangible items or finances, but the nurturance and guidance. We try to instill in them a spiritual presence at all times. As they make mistakes in life, most children look to their parents for direction. In an ideal world, they would always get back on the right path. In reality, they still depend on us as well as our prayers.

We begin to recognize the fact that regardless of the choices that our children make, our influence is appreciated to a great extent. Even though they might have complained about our seemingly stern efforts while they were at home, they come to the realization that our opinion matters. This occurs even when they're trying to function on their own.

One influence my parents instilled in me was to value education. They taught me how to work for what I want and to never let anyone or anything stand in my way. That taught me to look past fear and to explore new areas in life.

Finally, parents can teach their children invaluable lessons just by the way they handle everyday situations and how they respond to events. We can certainly receive both acclamation and confirmation from the Bible where parents receive guidance as well as assurance in Proverbs 22:6, *"Train up a child in the way he should go; even when he is old he will not depart from it."*

Chapter Seven

Pushed into Your Purpose

Many are the plans in a man's heart, but it is the Lords purpose that prevails. Proverbs 19:21

I can remember exactly when it happened... June 2018. I was sitting in my family room on a typical day after work...of course. I was feeling worn out and spiritually drained. Suddenly it hit me! I jumped up and said, "Michael, God just revealed the title of my book, "Hidden Realities." Ten minutes later, I was rattling off the chapters. It was just like that. Of course, it all happened when I was positioned in a new environment. It was one that forced me to get out of my comfort zone. It was a position where I was stretched spiritually, physically and emotionally. I welcomed it all because I knew exactly what my purpose was.

One of my favorite books is "Purpose Driven Life" by Pastor Rick Warren. He does an excellent job of helping readers to understand purpose and what it means. Pastor Rick Warren reminds us in his book, "Purpose Driven Life" that living on purpose is the only way to really live. Everything else is just existing. Most people struggle with three basic issues in life.

- The first is Identity. "Who am I?"
- The second is Importance: "Do I matter?"
- The third is Impact: "What is my place in life?"

Joel Osteen shared in a sermon, entitled, "Pushed into Your Purpose." What he goes on to explain is the reality that, we do not always understand why things happen to us in our life. Maybe you had a friend that you thought would be with you for years. This might have been somebody that you counted on for support. Suddenly, you had to move away and find new friends.

Maybe you were at work and things were going great. You had all this favor, but now there's conflict; everything's a struggle; and you stop enjoying our job. God knows we wouldn't go without a push and when everything is good, we are comfortable. We don't want to have to stretch. We don't want to have to find new friends and develop new skills. It is not our desire to get out of our comfort zones and step out into the unknown. We ask ourselves, "What if it doesn't work out?" We may not like the idea of what is happening, but if God had not closed those doors, we would've been satisfied to stay where we were.

When you're pushed into your purpose, it simply means that you are forced to realize not only what you're capable of but also recognizing your destiny and God's will. He knows what it is that you will become before you are able to decide for yourself. In my case, I had no intentions whatsoever of becoming a middle school principal. I realize now that I needed to experience this endeavor before arriving to my ultimate assignment.

God loves you and me too much to let us miss our destiny.

As a child of God, you have too much potential, too much talent, and too much in you to get stuck where you are. God will put us in difficult or uncomfortable situations that force us to stretch, and that will help us to grow.

Although I had some idea of what I would have liked to do next in my life, I could not be certain where my path would lead. I was all set to complete my final year in the Education field as Principal. Suddenly, I was redirected by God. He revealed to me that he was there to alleviate a great deal of my work load and much of the stress that I had endured for so many months. I had experienced health issues and needed to make a change. In addition, because of the impact of the demands on my life and my health, I was not functioning in the divine order in which I firmly believe — God first, then family, then work.

It was during my annual evaluation meeting when God whispered to me, once again, helping me to recognize the opportunity to request a less stressful position that would not only be better for my health, but allow me to operate in the divine order in which I believe.

Surprisingly, it was at that point that the words so effortlessly rolled from my tongue. I informed the leadership that I would appreciate it very much if they would consider allowing me to serve in a less-demanding position.

Now, I am able to feel a tremendous sense of inner peace. It is very important for me to be "purpose driven" in my assignment. I will be able to continuously impact the lives of both young children and adults in our community while being relieved from those *Hidden Realities* that were truly taking a toll on my life. I feel as if a heavy weight is being lifted from my shoulders. I know that I will experience less stress, minimal health issues, and hopefully eliminate those unforeseen periods of depression. You see, God needed me to let go of that which was not good for me.

However, I feel confident that the Lord will also have me to witness to others, particularly women, about my journey on this earth. I have no doubt that many will benefit from my selflessness in sharing both the positive and negative experiences. Often times when we are pushed into our purpose, we find ourselves standing alone. We realize that we have been isolated by God. He gets us alone so that we can hear his voice.

He sometimes uses loss, betrayal, and/or persecution that force us to make a change. God does not intend to make our lives miserable, but simply pushes us into our purpose. During my personal journey, I am able to determine when I am being pushed into my purpose. God shows me this when:

I. *Interruptions occur.*

I consider them to be divine interruptions. When I think every-thing is going well, I begin to experience interruptions in my life. When I am happy at home, there are interruptions. Even when I am happy at work, there are interruptions.

II. *I receive Strange Blessings.*

When I think of strange blessings, I do not only think of my situations. I am reminded of a close friend who lost her home during a recent hurricane in our small town. I remember it so well. The day after the storm, she called and said, "We lost everything."

My husband and I went to see how we could help. They were both in disbelief. It took weeks for them to wrap their heads around the situation. As time passed, they started to receive blessings in abundance. I had no doubt God had orchestrated this situation so that He could interrupt the process. He had to get them exactly where he wanted them to be in their walk with Him so that He could bless them in the way that He did.

III. *I begin to feel uncomfortable.*

Sometimes we are encouraged to get out of our comfort zone. There are other times when we automatically find ourselves in such situations. However, we begin to adjust and enjoy what we are doing. We begin to realize that we are actually making a difference in the lives of others. At that time, we suddenly understand that it was God who brought us to that place.

Prayer for purpose:

Heavenly Father, I pray that I may fulfill the work that You have purposed for me to do. I thank You Father that Your will for my life is to transform me into the image and likeness of the Lord Jesus Christ and I pray that my life may reflect His grace and beauty in all I say and do.

Chapter Eight

Knowing Your Worth

According to *Forbes Magazine*, Bill Gates is worth $102.1 Billion Dollars. Oprah Winfrey is worth $9.6 Billion Dollars and Steve Job's net worth was $10 Billion Dollars at the time of his death. So, how much are you worth? This is a personal question. Yes, these prominent individuals are worth an abundance in fame and fortune. Allow me to rephrase the question. Do you know your worth?

Yes, we should know our worth in the sense of who we are and what we have to offer relative to the spiritual realm. When we give advice to others we must consider, "Is the information that I am willfully sharing beneficial and from a positive mindset?" Forbes magazine points out in which successful companies take a great deal of time when calculating their value in the market. Knowing how much they are worth helps them expand, grow, and survive. Similarly, we as women should know our worth and know how to calculate our value. The article continues with ways in which women can become more worthy financially.

In this chapter, I want to stretch the thinking of women. You see, our value or worth is not about money or financial gain. In fact, I like this statement from the Forbes article; "We must align the core of who we are with the life skills we've acquired." If we stay true to our values and immune to other people's opinions of us, we can price ourselves more efficiently.

Allow me take this statement further: As women, we must know who we are and to whom we belong. As Christians, we must understand that a strong woman works out every day and takes pride in the appearance she portrays. As a woman of strength, she kneels to pray, keeping her soul in shape with God leading the way.

I believe it is important that we recognize self worth as what is inside of us rather than what we do or others see from the outside. We as women must not allow outside forces to define who we are or who we will become.

The world's standards are based upon external factors. However, women who know and understand their value focus on their internal factors.

Everyone has a special gift or talent, no matter how insignificant it may seem. Therefore, there is something that we are able to contribute that may be a tremendous task for other peers among us. On the contrary, through collaboration on a regular basis, we begin to recognize how we are able to benefit from others as well. Often times this occurs from merely through listening attentively.

If you don't believe in yourself and continuously feel that you are not capable of accomplishing whatever you set out to achieve, then no amount of motivation from others can benefit you. When you doubt yourself, you are actually focusing on negative aspects and those obstacles that may have previously been a hindrance. We must remain focused and be able to decipher which experiences we should reflect upon for guidance.

If someone truly values your services and you feel that you are capable of providing what they want, then an acceptable amount should be agreed upon by both parties.

Otherwise, the end result will not reflect the quality that might have been expected or deserved.

Whatever the case may be, we are not always able to determine the difference that we make for others. However, at some point someone may reveal how we unknowingly helped them or simply listened during a time when they felt the need for a small amount of attention. Ultimately, we will develop our strategic ability to truly become that light when someone may be in darkness.

No matter how others may decide to seek status or control, we must be true to what we believe. We all know of those who seemingly have no limits as to what they will do to quickly to get to the top. We have also witnessed how humility can serve as a major advantage, even in the workplace.

I want to share a few signs about value and worth by Morton Patterson (August 2017) Seven *Signs You Know Your Value and Self-Worth.*

Self-Worth Value # 1:
You have positive self-esteem.

You believe in and like yourself. Self-esteem is confidence in one's own worth or abilities. You are comfortable with who you are — your weight, height, and everything that makes and represents *you.*

You are confident in the work you deliver and your sense of professionalism. You like and have a great relationship with people. I think that without positive self-esteem it would be difficult to know your value.

Self-Worth Value # 2:
You recognize the difference you make.

When you know your value, you will confidently approach a negotiation with full belief in your knowledge, skills, experience, and the difference you can make.

Self-Worth Value # 3:
You see yourself as a peer.

Everyone has a special gift or talent, no matter how insignificant it may seem. Therefore, there is something that we are able to contribute that may be a tremendous task for other peers among us. On the contrary, through collaboration on a regular basis, we begin to recognize how we are able to benefit from others as well. Often times this occurs from merely through listening attentively.

In any given situation, knowing your value means feeling that you are an equal with anyone you interact with: clients, bosses, colleagues, or friends. You are not a supplicant. Nor do you feel privileged to be with someone or to work in a particular type of organization. You have a personal sense of value and deservedness and assert yourself as an equal in personal and business relationships.

Self-Worth Value # 4:
You do not undercharge for your services.

Quite often out of fear of losing business or the desire to win more business, people will undercharge for their services. This is a classic situation where they end up doing much more than they're paid to do. But, somehow, in a desire to prove themselves, these people still feel that they are not doing enough in relation to how much they are being paid.

This can set a precedent which could be hard to remove. Tepper recalls many years ago driving to a client's site and deep inside she was unhappy and annoyed. This was because she was hugely under-charging and unhappy with herself for continually doing so.

<u>Self-Worth Value # 5</u>:
You are clear about your values.

You know your boundaries. You are clear about what is acceptable behavior, how you like to be treated and spoken to, and you have the courage to speak out when necessary. You don't need external validation to prove your value — instead, you have an internal compass of what is right and wrong.

<u>Self-Worth Value # 6</u>:
You are engaged in work that is exciting and fulfilling.

When you are involved in work that is fulfilling as well as financially rewarding, you are more inclined to work with even greater commitment. I believe that when you love what you do, you are prepared to do more and to become more. However, if at least one other individual genuinely gains self-assurance from your efforts on his or her behalf, then the excitement will become even greater.

Chapter Nine

Women Strengthening Women

If I may, I would like to begin this chapter with a question? Why do we trip when we see other beautiful women? Why do we trip when other women are smarter or more successful than we are? Are you a hater or are you really insecure with yourself? My hope is that women can begin to strengthen other women by truly lifting them. You have to first know and understand who you are before you can lift or strengthen another woman. Understand that you are beautiful in your own way.

I remember being at an event among several beautiful women. They were all dressed up and appeared to be flawless. I said to one lady, "You are absolutely stunning!" I did not realize there was a gentleman standing near me. He walked over and said, "It takes a strong woman to tell another woman she is beautiful. He was exactly right. I have always believed in lifting other women. We need one another.

I am often reminded of how I feel when I am with my various groups of women. My college roommates are my friends for life. We have so many memories. Some are funny, some hurtful, and some memories are truly empowering. We have a deep rooted friendship. When we get together, it is like we pick up right where we left off. We have vowed to always be there for one another. We have watched each other blossom into strong women. We have shared many experiences. I am so glad God connected us.

My birthday club is another group of women who I adore. We meet several times a year and shower each other with love and gifts. We understand one another. This group is so real. We laugh, cry, and joke, but at the same time have an understanding that we are always there for one another. We are there to celebrate each other and to make women among the group feel special. Once we rented a hotel room and laughed like we never had before. We danced, sang, and enjoyed anything we wanted to eat. It was a night I will never forget. It was a night where women could be real with one another.

Women are usually rather sensitive in regard to several things that most likely seem unimportant to men. Therefore, only another woman can truly relate to what we as women feel. It will be beneficial as well for us to share with other women who possibly deal with the same experiences in life. The encouraging words of another woman may prevent a serious situation from occurring later. For this reason, we must share any experiences that will strengthen other women.

It is essential that we have women in our lives that are able to keep us grounded. I have several friends that I go to that are not in a specific group but are women who I can count on when I need them. These are women that I can have good conservations with. We do not engage in gossip. They listen and are available to me when I need to be uplifted. I know they have my back. I am thankful that God has provided me seasoned women who are full of wisdom as well. I have learned so much from women who can offer me wisdom. They enrich my life and help me through the process of becoming stronger.

This is similar to the process of becoming a Christian. Most of us started attending worship at a particular church as children. Later we were led and decided to join the church. We were soon taught that the church is actually in our heart and we simply joined a band of believers in Christ. Therefore, we entered our individual faith as "babes in Christ." We were also referred to as "new creatures" regarding what we believed. At that time, we were considered to be a novice when it came to understanding the word of God.

However, it quickly became someone's task to teach us more and more about the Lord. It may have been a Sunday School, Bible Study, or even a Vacation Bible School Teacher who gave us that extra motivation or desire to learn more. Today several churches have New Members Orientation. Generally, the Pastor would be tasked with meeting with those members for a few sessions.

Even after having consistently been a part of the church for several years, we continue to receive the nurturing that we need to become even more spiritually equipped. Therefore, we are able to offer some form of understanding to others who may either be new in Christ or are simply unable to interpret the word as we do. Whether it pertains to small children or adults, we can help strengthen the faith of others during our Christian journey or walk with Christ.

The same applies as we women strengthen other women. We are all equipped as we have undergone varying experiences throughout our lives that will surely be beneficial if shared with others. They need to understand that they too will be able to overcome whatever trying times they may face.

As we mature as women, we sometimes reflect on our past faults. We look back in amazement, wondering how we made it in life. Many times, it is the prayers of our mothers and other women who have been instrumental in our lives. Nonetheless, we have arrived at a place that should encourage us to continue to strengthen other women.

Our guidance could be an effort to prevent younger women from struggling and experiencing the same obstacles. Whether it is managing money, work related, spiritual guidance, or simply dealing with people, we as women should have some the wisdom that will cause other women to have a more productive future. It is our task to take the time to demonstrate concern as well as compassion for others. Sometimes we assume that we do not have any specific advice that will be of any value to someone else. However, we must be confident and realize that younger women are watching us and we should be role models and be in the business of building other women.

In my professional arena, I had several opportunities to pour into others, mostly women, as they strived to improve in various capacities. Through my continuous training and desire to help others, I was more aware of the tremendous potential among certain individuals.

Therefore, I was willing to assist those who humbly accepted guidance that I was willing to offer. Although my efforts were sometimes not welcomed, I could many times recognize a noticeable difference in those who embraced my level of expertise and wisdom.

It is a true process to grow into womanhood. You see, in order to get to a place where you can strengthen other women, you have to know who you are. You need to know *what makes you happy*. I myself will often times journal.

Once I tried to write at least ten things that make me happy. It was a struggle for me. Out of all the things that make me happy, just finding ten to write down became a challenge.

As I experienced life, my list got longer. Of course I could not be of any help to other women at that stage in my life because I did not really know what made me happy. I found myself looking at other women and what they had going on in order to help make me happy. I did a self-assessment early in my life which helped me to realize that I don't need anyone to validate me.

Women, we must stop looking for others to accept us. *God accepts us.* We must begin the business of strengthening women, not hurting them. When we walk into a room, we must walk in with full confidence. Know who we are. Know that we do not have to shrink because there are other beautiful women surrounding us. Be careful not to become part of shrinking other women. Some women do it only to make them self stand out. Women must acknowledge the thing that makes them a hater or what make them feel insecure, then deal with that thing. God cannot use us to strengthen other women when we are too busy finding fault in others. We need to focus on the process of becoming stronger. However, we must consider the following:

Speak up and not be quiet when it comes to building up other women.

We should take full advantage of every opportunity to help other women become stronger. We do not benefit from being selfish with our sharing of what made us become stronger as women.

Not shrink when we are surrounded by other beautiful women.

Know who you are. Know that you are beautiful in your own way. Set your own standards. Identify your own strength, then you will not be intimidated and feel the need to shrink in a room full of beautiful women. Besides, they might readily share some of their beauty tips.

Not engage in gossip about other women.

It should not be our task to bring down or belittle other women, or anyone but instead as Christians, we should lift them up and continuously offer them encouragement.

Not be jealous.

We should extend praise and possibly inquire positively about what we may desire. Jealousy is poison. Learn to like yourself and others at the same time. Try it! It can be done.

Live in our truth.

We must be true to ourselves and share with others while being real in the process. They should be able to recognize our genuine gestures.

Be accountable

In order to be accountable, we must be responsible with our actions with other women. It is essential that we are both honest and supportive in one another's goals. Most importantly, we should be uplifting.

Pray daily.

This will only make us stronger in all that we do for ourselves and in sharing with others, particularly women. Most importantly, prayer will keep us stronger day by day in our walk with God.

Chapter Ten

The Reality of Being a Godly Woman

When I think about a Godly woman, I think about her mind, body and soul. I think about her most inner being and what defines her. Who is she, really? I think about the role of the woman in the church, home and the workplace.

We as women have an inward ability to determine when we feel complete. We also know whether or not we are feeling that sense of accomplishment, based upon whether or not we have reached our goals in life. However, our individual goals are not by any means synonymous with our destiny. In order to recognize when we have reached that place that God intends for us to be, we must have a genuine relationship with him. It is that personal connection that will cause us to know that we truly feel complete.

A Godly woman represents the one who loves what she has become. She looks forward to awakening every morning to embark upon another day's journey. She is filled with joy in knowing that she is all that she desires to be. She feels content to know and understand that her life is pleasing in God's sight. So, naturally most women do not feel that they have actually arrived to such a point in life.

A Godly woman would to a large degree feel a need to be next to perfect. We can probably agree that this would be an unrealistic state. However, this is not to say that we should not strive to reach that status. On the other hand, as Christian women, we should have that special desire to become Godly. We should want to illuminate that marvelous light so that others will want to thrive for such outward contentment and self-assurance.

In today's society, Godly women sometimes are labeled as thinking they are somewhat "perfect." However, it is the goodness and strength within us that allow us to overlook the labels that follow us daily.

An actual occurrence happened at a local store in my hometown. A lady was approached by a fairly young man who asked, "Ma'am, are you a Christian?" She immediately and proudly replied, "I am!" He suddenly began to share the fact that he had not been living as he should. He proceeded to express his desire for the lady to help him and lead him down the right path. In fact, he asked her to save him. Knowing she understood only God saves and this seemed rather farfetched; she somehow felt an overwhelming sense of obligation to minister to him. She simply articulated the fact that it was his task to first believe in God, the Father. She went on to let him know that he has to believe within his heart and confess it aloud that Jesus is all powerful and can truly deliver him from any evil. Surprisingly, the young man began to inquire about the church she attended.

You see, it was her aura and countenance that generated so powerfully that day. We need to be mindful of how we carry ourselves. What are others seeing in us? Is our light shining? We must stand out in a crowd.

So, what then does a Godly woman represent? We see ourselves as the portrayal of righteousness without conceit and boastfulness. We are wise in our own rite. It is our desire to please God as we represent him in our daily walk. We do not wish to tear others down, but recognize the good in them and strive to influence those who will listen.

In our homes we are looked up to among our family members. They demand respect from others who are in our presence. We set an example of kindness, generosity, and patience.

I can remember when I struggled with being submissive to my husband. I had a sort of bossy demeanor. Little did I know, I was choosing a position that felt stressful, uneasy and out of order. In fact, I was out of divine order.

I was reminded of 1 Peter 3:1 Wives, in the same way submit yourselves to your own husbands so that, if any of them do not believe the word, they may be won over without words by the behavior of their wives,

When I think of a Godly woman in the home, she is submissive. By this I mean, she is respectful to her husband. She believes in him and has no problem honoring him. She is protective of him and yes, she obeys him while allowing him to lead. Allow me to be honest. Initially, during the first few years of marriage. I had to grow in my spiritual walk to better understand my role as a wife and as a Godly woman.

I remember reading the book, "The Power of a Praying Wife, by Stormie Omartian. The book was a blessing to me. This book helped me to seek out hidden areas in my heart that was unhealthy. I also embraced my role as a Godly woman, that is to ensure I did all I could to have an orderly home. Now, that I have grown spiritually over the years, my prayer and testimony is for women to become more submissive so that they can reap the benefits of a wholesome, happy marriage as Godly women.

Mary Powell took a closer look by examining a few characteristics of a Godly Woman:

1. SEEK GOD FIRST: It is important for us to understand that anything and everyone cannot satisfy us. *"But seek first His kingdom and His righteousness, and all these things will be added to you. So do not worry about tomorrow; for tomorrow will care for itself. Each day has enough trouble of its own."* – Matthew 6:33-34 (NASB)

2. SPEAK FAITHFULLY: Love others with godly wisdom, boldness, and kindness as a faithful completer of others. *"She opens her mouth in wisdom, and the teaching of kindness is on her tongue."* – Proverbs 31:26 (ESV)

3. SHOW TRUE BEAUTY: Bodies deteriorate; persons develop. Invest in that which lasts. Powell expresses her feeling of being in a battle every day— a constant struggle of having to deal with the expectations of the world in regard to her walk as a Christian.

Powell hopes that one day, in God's strength and grace, we can truly be free from this battle as women. *"And do not be conformed to this world, but be transformed by the renewing of your mind, that you may prove what is that good and acceptable and perfect will of God"* (Romans 12:2 NKJV).

She reminds us that Proverbs 31:30 lets us know that beauty is "vain" and we can be beautiful on the outside and, most importantly, on the inside. I believe that it is not our desire, as Godly women to allow ourselves to become conceited in our efforts to maintain our beauty. As you attempt to be all the woman you can be and achieve the great things you know you are destined for, Peter Jones shares a few things you can try to increase your chances.

When I think of a Godly woman, I am reminded of many women in my circle. I especially think about the woman who sits next to me almost every Sunday for years now. I believe that she is the epitome of a Godly woman. She can almost sense when something is going wrong with me. She exudes a love that is heartfelt and genuine. Her smile is piercing and her demeanor is a model for other Christian women.

There is something about a Godly woman that stands out. She shines from the inside out. She has a positive attitude and perspective on life. Her personality effortlessly draws others toward her. She does not only talk the talk, but walks the walk.

Descriptions of a Godly Woman

Devoted to God

A woman who is devoted to God finds her purpose and her identity. As she allows God to pour into her, Christ begins to shine through her. She then pours into her husband, her children, and others.

Faith

A woman of faith will not be moved. No matter how she feels or what others say, she stands firm on her faith. Her faith is what drives her heart, and then leads her to her destiny.

Discernment

A Godly woman has a spiritual filter that separates the good from the bad. She prays and asks God for discernment and applies it to her daily living. She also uses it to cover her family as well as her surroundings.

A Godly Woman is a good wife

She will never speak negatively about her husband to her children, family, friends or co-workers. A good wife is one who takes care of her family.

Finally, as Godly women, we know our boundaries in regard to our families and other relationships. The Lord is continuously leading us as we never stop seeking his direction. It should be clearly evident that he is always present in our lives.

Biography

Letitia Parrish Austin

Photo courtesy of Vonda Hubbard

While tackling challenging obstacles and unprecedented phases in her life, Letitia Parrish Austin has withstood both Depression and Anxiety while experiencing varying "Hidden Realities" along the way. Such Realities are revealed in this spiritual account as it provides genuine counsel for women who may be dealing with similar issues.

In the midst of a career that appeared to be everything that she had hoped for; life brought about a turn of events that most would recognize as positive. In the process, she received "Teacher of the Year" two times on the Elementary Level, Model Classroom status four times and was named "Most Influential Teacher" several times by Honor Students. Nonetheless, Austin escalated from an

Elementary School Teacher to a successful Middle School Principal in her hometown while simultaneously dealing with spiraling emotions of loneliness, confusion, uncertainty and grief, to name a few. In spite of it all, Austin also finds time to serve as a Part-time Instructor from a well-known University.

Letitia Austin is very active in her church and she faithfully serves in several capacities, including the Vision Team. She is noted for inspiring other women through speaking at various churches where she addresses her personal coping and shares encouraging words to strengthen others. Her unwavering conviction is that we as women are able to empower one another.

Austin once wrote an insert for a play entitled; "Behind the Mask" where she depicted women who hide behind the mask of makeup, clothes, smiles, etc. to deal with the demands of the world and the workforce. However, she is most proud of being named 2013 Bainbridge Living Magazine "Women to Watch," where she appeared on the front cover.

Although her ongoing journey is one that causes her to balance family, ministry and work, Austin welcomes the challenge with Grace, integrity and dignity. She believes that her life is purpose–driven as she is constantly guided by God's divine plan which she has no doubt will lead to her destiny. Her favorite quote is "Each Day We Earn our Wings."

Austin is married to Deacon Michael Austin of 25 years. The two of them are blessed with two children, Taylor and Corbin. She has been an educator in the local county school system for 29 years. Austin is also an active member of a wealth of educational organizations.